Copyright © 2021 by Wayne Pratt

All rights reserved. No part of this publication may be reproduced, distributed, or transmitted in any form or by any means, including photocopying, recording, or other electronic or mechanical methods, without the prior written permission of the publisher, except in the case of brief quotations embodied in critical reviews and certain other noncommercial uses permitted by copyright law.

Requests for permission to make copies of any part of the work should be sent to Wayne Pratt at: wayne@waynepratt.ca

Publisher:
Motive8u Inc., 829 Norwest Road, Suite 424, Kingston, Ontario, Canada K7P2N3

Title: **31 Days** or *Tips to help you get from where you are to where you want to be.*

Format: Paperback

Author: Wayne Pratt

Illustrations : Ophelia Verk

ISBN 978-1-7777184-0-4

First printing: 15 October 2019

Second Revision: 20 July 2021

31 DAYS

or

Tips to help you get from where you are to where you want to be.

Wayne Pratt

Illustrations by Ophelia Verk

Index

1. Don't hire a broke Success Coach — 1
2. The depressed motivator — 3
3. How to make a difference here and now — 5
4. What do you do? — 8
5. Someday Isle — 10
6. To Be, Do, Have — 13
7. Motive8u — 15
8. Looking for community — 17
9. It is hard to start a business today — 19
10. Intrapreneuring — 22
11. Mental Illness — 25
12. Now what? — 28
13. Career Advice — 31
14. Coaching… The Movie — 34
15. Purpose & Packaging — 36
16. Happy New Year! — 39
17. So I lost my Uncle… — 41
18. Why Businesses Fail — 43
19. Spinning your wheels — 46
20. So you won — 48
21. At the cottage — 50
22. Sharpen the saw — 52
23. Self-Confidence — 54
24. Own your goals! — 58
25. Plan for bad days — 60
26. Celebrate the wins — 63
27. Gratitude — 65
28. Find your hidden talents and skills — 67
29. Looking back — 69
30. What do you do when things go wrong? — 72
31. Become an Overcomer! — 74

So you want to be coached? — 77

You can reach me at *wayne@waynepratt.ca*

1

Don't hire a broke Success Coach

There is a fair amount of information floating around about "Success Coaching". My brother, who is a pastor, says the growth in interest is simply because some people who don't go to church, still want a sermon.

I have some opinions/suggestions which may or may not fit you.

1. Never hire a broke Success Coach.

2. Never hire someone you don't like. This seems obvious, but some coaches think they are Drill Sergeants.

3. That said, remember, if they don't hold you accountable, you are merely renting a friend.

What were your thoughts on the last chapter?

Is there something you read which you thought might benefit you if you implemented it in your life?

2

The depressed motivator

Did you hear about the man who wanted to be a motivator but was too depressed? At first it is funny, but on another level there is a real truth here.

The real test of a trainer/motivator is how do they act when the stage lights are off? As they say – you shouldn't trust a vegetarian butcher.

There are those in our industry who view their clients as rubes, and believe their job is done when the snake oil is delivered. The rest of us struggle with trying to balance living with integrity while admitting we are human and our smiles are not surgically pasted to our faces…

All people have to face the ebb and flow of day-to-day life. Some manage this more gracefully then others. A positive, goal focused person will bounce back quicker from events that stop others, and perhaps even use the circumstance as a learning tool.

Some folks say the glass is half empty, others say it is half full. But the people who seem to have the most satisfaction in their lives are the ones who say: "Wow, that glass needs to be filled up!" and then set about filling it.

I'm still trying to be a glass-filling kind of guy – the jury's still out on that, but I keep trying.

What were your thoughts on the last chapter?

Is there something you read which you thought might benefit you if you implemented it in your life?

3

How to make a difference here and now

Do you feel stuck? Are you bored and frustrated? Are you at the lottery counter twice a week?

I may have a solution! Do your job, get good at it, and spend X hours a week striving at what ever the dream is.

Today there is no disrespect for the bi-vocational worker. We are all contractors now. As far as the "dream" goes, you can almost always do something towards the big goal every week, however incremental. In fact, I believe regularly striving toward and revising your goals is the difference between a wish and a goal.

When you read a business newspaper, you are told again and again how business is changing. To riff on Marty McFly from the movie "Back to the Future" I believe there is a solution.

It is loosely based on the old system of guilds. But we have to accept the fact that the post-industrial age business model we knew from the fifties and sixties is gone. Get over it.

Do you have a craft or talent? Do you have a computer? A phone? The 40,000 square feet factory, the walls of file cabinets, and the steno pool have all been replaced.

What will it take for us to stop romancing the past, and actually produce something? Do you want to raise sheep? Spin wool? Make sweaters? Sell sweaters? Here's an update on those ancient guilds – we can (and do) form our own much smaller and more specialized guilds.

What were your thoughts on the last chapter?

Is there something you read which you thought might benefit you if you implemented it in your life?

_____
_____
_____
_____
_____
_____
_____
_____
_____

You can reach me at *wayne@waynepratt.ca*

4

What do you do?

As a public speaker, I am often asked, "So what do you do?" Or – "How do you motivate me?" I will let you in on a secret; all permanent change comes from within. My job is either, to entertain or at best, help you decide what it is you want.

I believe it was J.P. Morgan who said "All goal setting is simple, decide what you want, decide what price you must pay, and resolve to pay that price. All else is corollary."

The real tragedy is so few have decided what it is they want. One issue I believe strongly in, is that healthy goal setting is more than just stuff. Toys and perhaps some travel are nice, but what you want to be is far more important than what you want to have.

With the near collapse of the North American banking system, some people are getting off the treadmill, and asking themselves "what do I want to be when I grow up"? Please let me know if you find an answer, or if I can help you get there.

What were your thoughts on the last chapter?

_____
_____
_____
_____
_____
_____
_____
_____

Is there something you read which you thought might benefit you if you implemented it in your life?

_____
_____
_____
_____
_____
_____
_____
_____
_____

You can reach me at *wayne@waynepratt.ca*

5

Someday Isle

Summer seems to be coming in earnest, so I assume some are off to Someday Isle. I first heard this concept from Dennis Waitley, which is to postpone your future by offering to do the things you have talked and dreamed of "someday" – as in "someday I'll…"

What is on your Someday Isle list? It is to travel? To write a book? Start that company? I have been working on my own list as well – remember Mime Radio?

I have, however, come up with the biggest difference between the delivered and the permanently wished for. It is simple, but not necessarily easy.

How can you spend twenty minutes a day working toward your goal? And are you willing?

What were your thoughts on the last chapter?

Is there something you read which you thought might benefit you if you implemented it in your life?

You can reach me at *wayne@waynepratt.ca*

6

To Be, Do, Have

When I was a much younger, I was so into the stuff I was going to have.

I would have it, then I could do it, and lastly, be it.

I did not know I had it completely backward.

What is even *more* scary, is that the North American culture got it backward.

I am not against aspirational marketing. However, our first goal should be to *be* whatever we are striving for and let the do's and the haves take care themselves.

I was in Niagara Falls N.Y. last week, and I got thinking about the differences between the two countries. One difference is, for the most part, if you discuss a business incubator, people in Ontario think you are talking about raising chickens. So what am I talking about?

A business incubator is an environment where start ups can receive office space, often mentoring, a variety of office equipment and services, and perhaps more importantly, other business people to talk to and often get feedback.

Much of Silicon Valley (Southern California) was and is built on this model. Even financing is often part of the package.

So why are they relevant? Well, besides not reinventing the wheel, and getting twenty photocopiers, and twenty water coolers, it not only manages cost, but it lets us function in the tribe, where productivity and protection work together.

If you have read any of my previous posts, you can imagine the demographic that I would like to bring together to grow individual and social goals. If this makes sense to you, I could use some more flag wavers.

What were your thoughts on the last chapter?

Is there something you read which you thought might benefit you if you implemented it in your life?

_____
_____
_____
_____
_____
_____
_____
_____
_____
_____

7

Motive8u

As a person who has worked closely with goal setting and the motivational training industry, I am getting concerned with our total preoccupation with "toy" consumption.

I have long coached using visuals to represent the achievement of a clear set and aspired goal. However, I think the car, boat, watch etc. should be a reflection of the service provided by the goal setter to better the client, perhaps the world. I have no time or use for the "occupy" movement, however what appears to them as moral bankruptcy may be putting the emphasis on the wrong syllable. *It makes more sense said than read.*

Can I be bold and recommend that our search for significance be more than the accumulation of stuff?

If you have a skill, body of knowledge, trade or asset base which produces more than a living, I am all for enjoying the things life can bring. Focus on mastery, and the bling will take care of itself.

What were your thoughts on the last chapter?

Is there something you read which you thought might benefit you if you implemented it in your life?

8

Looking for community

I just came back from Cincinnati. Looking at buying into an executuve coaching franchise, I truly drank the grape juice.

I realized what I was hoping for was two things; a chance to impart things I have learned, and an opportunity to build community.

I am not into sports, and I am not into bars. Small business seems like my community. Working with a group of business people to mutually grow each other, I believe is my calling. It may sound naïve, but that's the dream.

What were your thoughts on the last chapter?

Is there something you read which you thought might benefit you if you implemented it in your life?

9

It is hard to start a business today…

I sometimes hear it is so hard to start a business today. I find this fascinating! I believe it has never been easier.

Look at your cell phone. You can be reached and reach out anywhere. You're no longer stuck in a ten by twelve box, waiting, because somebody said they would call.

Speaking of phones, I am guessing you have a smart phone. My phone, not high end by the way, has more computing power than my first three computers. With the Internet and Google, the information you are looking for is probably at your fingertips. With outsourcing, miniaturization and even 3 D printing, plants and offices that took thousands of square feet and thousands of dollars in rent, are now in second bedrooms. Wow!

The three main ingredients to launching a new business are still an idea, passion and a lot of persistence.

In a previous post, I alluded to the movie "Back to the Future". Well, I'm at it again.

This "new" idea was published first in 1937. I am referring to Napoleon Hill's seminal work, *Think and Grow Rich*.

This book, with *How to Win Friends and Influence People* by Dale Carnegie, are in my opinion the two must read books of the 20th Century.

The point I want to feature here in Hill's book, is the "Master Mind Group" Why is it still relevant? It is the last century's answer to social networking.

I offer two observations. First, and more important than it might seem having peers whom you like and trust can help prevent the loneliness and self doubt that small business can bring.

Second – signal to noise ratio. By which I mean to say; Google or Twitter may offer 100,000 hits from random strangers, but the people you like and trust can probably offer more thoughtful help and encouragement.

So, find four to six peers, meet weekly, discuss challenges you are having, where you are going, celebrate your wins, and keep good notes!

What were your thoughts on the last chapter?

Is there something you read which you thought might benefit you if you implemented it in your life?

You can reach me at *wayne@waynepratt.ca*

10

Intrapreneuring

Many people have struggled with employment, and several dream of being an entrepreneur, but that too has its pitfalls. May I suggest another option?

Become an intrapreneur.

– What's an intrapreneur? Simply put, they don't work for, they work with. Instead of an employer, you have a client.

– You control your time, you supervise yourself, you own your tools, and the client gets the result they contracted for.

– For example, you contract to clean a parking lot for $20.00. You show up Tuesday night with a broom and garbage bags spend two hours, bill the client, and get $20.00. Next Tuesday show up, spend 6 hours, it is the same $20.00.

– Is that fair? I don't know, but it is commerce. It also shows how important understanding your costing, including your time, is.

Why Bother?

– More sense over the control of your time.

– Less time with soul sucking middle management.

– The ability to make more money without groveling

– Up to 20-30 percent reduction in income tax costs (seek accounting help).

– Maybe a shoe in to an opportunity you could not have gotten as an employee.

What risks are there?

– You have no employee benefits.

– You have to have the discipline to do the book keeping to survive.

– Revenue Canada can undo your status and claim you are an employee. Have your ducks in a row.

– You have to be prepared to think like an owner. It is not all champagne and cigars.

———————

What were your thoughts on the last chapter?

You can reach me at *wayne@waynepratt.ca*

Is there something you read which you thought might benefit you if you implemented it in your life?

11

Mental Illness

I risk going off topic today. I often speak about goal setting or small business, but statistics tell us mental illness affects one in five families, so this affects business, it affects goal setting, and it affects life.

First question. Why are we so frightened of people with a mental illness? I have some thoughts, first, it makes good TV. The deranged killer, the crippling delusions, the lack of affect or compassion, on the spectrum not very representative, but it can fill the theatre.

Secondly, we only see this community during an "episode" possibility the worst two or three weeks of their life, but not their life.

And lastly, I think it interferes with what we think normal is. We often want things the same, and depending on the illness, same just isn't possible.

So what can we do? I think the biggest breakthrough would be to stop "all or nothing" thinking. If he or she has trouble getting or keeping a job, let's find them a welfare apartment, and a disability cheque, and maybe, just maybe there might be enough for a case of beer at the end of the month.

We seem to forget that ten months a year, they were good sculptors, painters, carpenters, etc. Are there people whose illness has so crippled them that a rooming house and a welfare cheque is as good as it is going to get? Sadly, yes, but we should not have this be the default.

What were your thoughts on the last chapter?

Is there something you read which you thought might benefit you if you implemented it in your life?

12

Now what?

A logical question is "now what"? What can we do differently within the current financial and social constraints in order to accomplish "what"?

I believe I have a solution to part of the problem: self-employment. Yes – self-employment.

Now, before you go all "One Flew Over the Cuckoo's Nest" on me, it should be understood that current treatments and new drug therapies have provided more autonomy and independence to the "consumer" than ever before. (Isn't that a stupid term? Like "I would like a cup of mental illness, please"?)

What has *not* changed as much, is society's need to infantilize those who suffer from mental illness. A retort I once heard speaks this clearly, "I am nuts, not stupid!"

Here is where I state that there are some people with some illnesses, who will not be able to work 40 to 50 hours a week at the same employer for five years or more. So what? As I alluded to before, there's no reason we have to immediately jump to a disability check, a welfare apartment and a lifetime of learned helplessness.

So you can ask, why are you preaching self-employment?

In an earlier post, I mentioned that business is not just 100's of thousands of square feet of offices, and 1000's of factory workers making widgets. Today, a man or woman with a skill and a cell phone, and maybe a laptop, can do more than legions of the business people of our past. Whether developing software or plowing snow, there are things people can and want to do. So the real question is what can we do to help?

What were your thoughts on the last chapter?

Is there something you read which you thought might benefit you if you implemented it in your life?

13

Career Advice

When Dustin Hoffman was the Graduate in that famous 60's movie, he was given one word as career advice, that word was "plastics". If I was offering *two* words for the next generation they would be "second career".

Many people dream of retiring at sixty-five. So if you retire at sixty-five and live till eighty-five or ninety, what can you productively do for much of those twenty or twenty five years? Golf becomes work after two or three games a week, and most people find travel, when a full time diet, gets old.

So what is there to do? My personal suggestion is to go back to that "Someday I'll…." list. Everyone has one. Is there a career that you dreamed of but just never had the courage or the right timing to do? Astronaut or ballerina might be out of the question, but really, what have you got to lose? So, what are your gifts?

What do I mean? Have you ever listened to a musician, and thought he or she is gifted? Well, music is only one of several gifts, and you probably have one or two you are strong in. If you want to know more, go to Google, type in "gifting seminars", and find one to take!

Too many people picked a career because someone in grade ten told them that's where the jobs were. We raised an entire society of people paid well to hate their jobs. This maybe your chance to do what you love, To quote the great Wayne Gretzy – "*You always miss 100% of the shots you never take.*"

What were your thoughts on the last chapter?

Is there something you read which you thought might benefit you if you implemented it in your life?

_____
_____
_____
_____
_____
_____
_____
_____
_____
_____

14

Coaching… The Movie

So…what's happening with my potential coaching career?

Well, here is my prediction: Coaching will almost completely replace motivational training over the next few years.

The largest reason? Well, aside that coaching is the flavour of the month, the main criticism of much motivational training, you go to the course, get excited, take notes, make promises to yourself, go home, wake up in the same bed with the same job, the same family, and the recycling to put out, and yesterday's course and all those changes you said you were going to make go right out the window.

With coaching, you have at least a chance to build new habits to make those goals you wrote down at the course, at least a possibility. And no, business coaching doesn't involve a whistle.

I don't know completely what form this new project will take, but I promise to keep you briefed.

What were your thoughts on the last chapter?

Is there something you read which you thought might benefit you if you implemented it in your life?

You can reach me at *wayne@waynepratt.ca*

15

Purpose & Packaging

Today's note is about two things, purpose and packaging. If you have been following me for a while, you know I like to help people be all they can be. The other part of the puzzle is the packaging. What would create an environment where I could do well by doing good? A friend and I recently rediscovered Napoleon Hill's seminal work, *Think and Grow Rich*.

Hill spends much of the book discussing a concept he referred as the Master Mind group.

It is simply, a small group of usually four to six people, committed to the wellbeing of the fellow members and developing opportunities and solving problems with each other, and in turn gaining new insights on their own situation. He believed that if the right people were chosen, it was almost like there was another mind at work helping solve these problems beyond the finite capabilities of the group. Therefore; The Mastermind.

Countless groups have been prospering with these tools, including such luminaries as Jack Canfield (Mr. Chicken Soup)

We wondered; what would make this powerful material more up to date? We think we got it. Combine this timeless work with the power and speed of the Internet. Independent of geography and venues, without even finding a parking space. Using the power of Skype and our proprietary website, the hour you spend in the meeting is an hour you spend developing you and your future, not discussing last nights ball game or the weather.

What were your thoughts on the last chapter?

Is there something you read which you thought might benefit you if you implemented it in your life?

_____
_____
_____
_____
_____
_____
_____
_____
_____
_____

16

Happy New Year!

Over the next few days we enter one of the most self-destructive times of the whole year. I refer to New Year's resolutions. We willingly agree to take on long reams on arguably "better lifestyle" goals only to drop them defeated and filled with self loathing by the first of February. I have something that might be more successful. If where you are is not where you want to be, pick one to three things, NO MORE. Then spend thirty to forty-five minutes a week making those things better. You aren't stuck, you aren't overwhelmed, and you don't hate your self in February. Give it a try.

What were your thoughts on the last chapter?

Is there something you read which you thought might benefit you if you implemented it in your life?

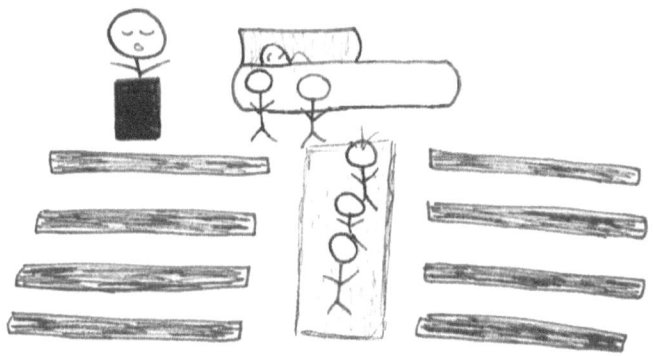

17

So I lost my Uncle…

I lost my uncle last week, Harry Pratt. He was truly the most civic minded man I ever met. As well, I was blown away by the profound outpouring of grief in his community. They even lowered the flags on the hospital! I was remembering Steve Covey's book "7 Habits of Highly Effective People". Begin with the end in mind. He proposes thinking about your funeral. What do you want said about you? What would your family say? What would your work colleagues say? Your community acquaintances? Are these thoughts positive and uplifting? If not, what do you have to change to have it be so? Good luck on changing these scripts.

What were your thoughts on the last chapter?

Is there something you read which you thought might benefit you if you implemented it in your life?

18

Why Businesses Fail

I am often asked why businesses fail. Although there can be specifics, most businesses seem to fail for the same reasons:

• Misunderstanding the need. Many new business people think if they want a good or service, everyone wants that good or service. Not necessarily. There are many great books on prototyping or a process called failing fast that let you test the marketplace, i.e. don't sign a five year lease because you have a neat idea.

• Too many fixed expenses for the sales you create. Or to boil it down, rent and capital costs kill.

• Spending the gross. This is such an easy trap to fall in. The most obvious example is throwing the sales tax collected into your business bank account and leaving it there. The temptation to view it as revenue is overwhelming. Get it into a separate tax account! The second part of this ditch is confusing revenue with income. Income comes from what is left after replacement costs, depreciation, government and industry fees, etc. I have met too many $100,000 income earners who had to go bankrupt because they ignored this simple rule.

• Not putting anything side to make needed capital or operational changes. Businesses are changing daily so don't be the last to know.

What were your thoughts on the last chapter?

Is there something you read which you thought might benefit you if you implemented it in your life?

You can reach me at *wayne@waynepratt.ca*

19

Spinning your wheels

Are you spinning you wheels? Are you bogging down? Is it hard to get started? These discussions usually are about winter, but what about us? May I recommend a finance tool; zero based thinking. This simply means if you would not be doing what you are doing now, stop doing it. Now hold on, I am not suggesting quitting your job, or leaving your husband, but how about taking a course? Converting a hobby into a business? Develop time-lines for exiting that dead-end position? I think you will find, once you start making these decisions, you will feel more hopeful and likely more purposeful.

What were your thoughts on the last chapter?

Is there something you read which you thought might benefit you if you implemented it in your life?

20

So you won...

North Americans love lotteries. So, what if your lottery ticket won? After too much to eat and drink, and maybe some travel, now what?

Do you want to give some away? Would you fund a small business? Would you go back to school?

Now the shocker; you can do most of these things without the ticket. The ticket you have is time and priorities. It will be slower, maybe less colourful, but drive, focus and a sense of purpose can have you achieving the same list as that winning list. Here is the homework. Write down three items that were on that lottery list and put time lines on what you hope to achieve and what are you doing to do next week to get this process started. Let me know what you thought about this process.

What were your thoughts on the last chapter?

Is there something you read which you thought might benefit you if you implemented it in your life?

You can reach me at *wayne@waynepratt.ca*

21

At the cottage

I write this blog staring past the computer at Dog Lake. We have moved to the Rideau River, September 1. If you have known me a while, you know that living by the water has been a goal of mine for a very long time.

So how did this come about?

My mother who had the property, is getting married, and is moving back to the city. So an offer was made to me. You see, setting your mind on what you want, and develop the how separately, is a lot more productive that merely to stop dreaming.

What were your thoughts on the last chapter?

Is there something you read which you thought might benefit you if you implemented it in your life?

You can reach me at *wayne@waynepratt.ca*

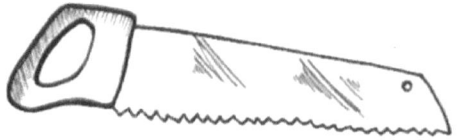

22

Sharpen the saw

Today I continue the series on starting a small business, a process I call micropreneuring. A crucial step comes from Stephen Covey's book the "7 Habits of Highly Effective People". I refer to "sharpen the saw". It tells of a man who sets out to cut trees. The first day he cuts two cords of wood. The next day he cut less than a cord, and on the third day barely half a cord. A neighbour asked if he had sharpened the saw, he said he did not have time as there was too much wood to cut. We can be like that lumberjack. So how do we sharpen the saw? Get enough sleep, read things that interest us, especially wisdom literature. Hobbies, sports, and our communities, all sharpen the saw. Go back at it refreshed and relaxed and you will be amazed how much more wood you can cut!

What were your thoughts on the last chapter?

Is there something you read which you thought might benefit you if you implemented it in your life?

23

Self-Confidence

Everything seems easier when you're brimming with self-confidence. *Self-confidence provides a solid foundation for living a life of happiness and accomplishing great things.* Unfortunately, it seems like the world is doing everything in its power to destroy whatever self-confidence you might enjoy.

Your opinion of yourself shapes your beliefs, behaviours, and outcomes.

Enjoy more self-confidence and the benefits it provides:

Start small. If your self-confidence is lacking, start small. There are many simple things you can do that make a difference. Here are a few:

– Get a new haircut that makes you look your best.

– Dress well.

– Get your car washed and detailed.

– Smile.

Limit your negative self-talk. Notice the negative things you say to yourself and quickly edit them into a more positive version. ***This requires time and energy, but the payoff is huge.***

Volunteer. You'll be proud of yourself if you get out of the house and do something for someone else. You might even make a new friend or two, which can also build your self-confidence. As an added bonus, volunteering is free of charge.

Try to prepare. Whether you have a presentation at work, a date, or a party on the social horizon, be prepared. Wear clothes that fit the occasion. Who will be there? What do you need to know? How can you best prepare? You'll feel much more confident when you're highly prepared.

Set a small goal and achieve it. Nothing builds confidence like success, so make success easy. Choose a small, yet meaningful, goal and ensure you achieve it. Enjoy the success. You'll have the confidence to go after a bigger goal next time.

A steady stream of victories is the surest way to boost your self-confidence. You'll feel like there's nothing you can't do.

Make a list of your strengths, talents, and accomplishments. Rather than focusing on the things you don't do well, spend some time being positive. Grab a pen and a piece of paper.

– What are your greatest achievements?

– What do you do well?

– What are your strengths?

Make a list. You'll be amazed by how amazing you are.

Avoid comparisons to others. Sure, your cousin makes more money. Your neighbour is more attractive. Your boss drives a better car. It's easy to find someone doing better in some small way. Instead of comparing yourself to others, compare yourself to yourself. Have you gained or lost weight since last month? How has your bank account changed since last year?

Focus on your personal progress and forget about making comparisons to others.

A high level of self-confidence makes every part of life easier. Create a strong foundation for achieving those big goals by taking the actions required to boost your confidence and self-esteem. Self-confidence gives you the power to change your life.

Remember, the prize often goes not to the better person, but to the more confident person.

What were your thoughts on the last chapter?

Is there something you read which you thought might benefit you if you implemented it in your life?

24

Own your goals!

This is a hobby horse of mine. I think people are not owning their goals. I have a friend who spent a year and a half flirting with alcoholism so he could avoid becoming a lawyer, which was his girlfriend's dream for him. The miserable doctor whose father was a doctor and made it clear that was what was expected, is almost a metaphor. Not only fathers and girlfriends, but our culture also tries to force their choices and opinions on us. I have another friend who believes success is flying around in private jets. And because he can't, he does nothing. The most specific example which effects my clients, is goal setting for people with disabilities. No one wants to feel stupid, or a slacker, so when they compare themselves to others or other people's goals they just give up. I recommend setting small goals, achieve them, and then stack them, so that big goals don't seem that surprising. Try it! Spend an hour setting some personal goals for you. Let me know how it went.

What were your thoughts on the last chapter?

Is there something you read which you thought might benefit you if you implemented it in your life?

You can reach me at *wayne@waynepratt.ca*

25

Plan for bad days

This blog you are not going to hear many other places. It is called, "plan for bad days".

There is a myth out there that if you are not hard driving seventy hours a week, you are just not in business. And unlike the Easter Bunny or the Tooth Fairy this myth is crippling lives. I coach several people with illnesses and disabilities, and they tell me "measuring up" is one of their biggest fears. I ask them, measuring up to what? Their goal set? Their client's expectations? Their trusted advisors expectations? Whether they are on the cover of Fortune Magazine is not a criteria.

Can you only work three days a week and stay well? Then work three days! Do you need to move an appointment because the path from your door to the bus stop seems one hundred miles?

Make sure you make the next one then move it! Make sure your face time with customers is quality time. If you are worried your goal sheet is a little light, not a problem, get those goals achieved and then set bigger ones. You don't have to compare yourself to any one you are not likely to hear the theme of this blog from too many "success coaches" or hear preached from many motivational speakers, but I believe is very important none the less. We currently live in an all or nothing world. If we can't fly around in G5's (an executive jet) we are just bums and should be happy in our basement apartments. Or to put it another way, if I can't make $100,000 per year, why even try? Now before every trainer and coach in North America brands me a heretic, let me state clearly, I very much believe in goals and stretch goals and even goals others consider huge. I just don't believe driving your ship into the rocks because it worked out differently than you hoped. Did you learn anything? Have you grown personally in the process? Have you set new goals driven by your new wisdom that have a much better chance a fulfillment?

One of my personal passions is coaching people who society deem "disabled". My biggest challenge is not helping them consider how they might be able to more productively use their time, in a small business, charity or whatever. It is getting them passed the learned helplessness that they may have developed. Can they build something that means something to them? Can they make five phone calls to prospects even though their phone feels like it is five hundred pounds? Do we applaud these people? No, we tell them it is too risky, or that their business is not "real" or perhaps, if we are government agencies, we threaten to claw back dollar for dollar what little remuneration they have made! Okay, I will get off my soap box now, but if you think I making sense, shoot me an e-mail.

What were your thoughts on the last chapter?

Is there something you read which you thought might benefit you if you implemented it in your life?

26

Celebrate the wins

In my twenty-five years of helping people with small businesses, I find most did not plan or expect the various setbacks endemic in self-employment. Several seemed to quit just before the finish line. So what can we do? I believe the secret is celebrating the wins, and not just the out of the park hits. The small incremental successes by their very nature add up. So how do you celebrate? Is it a Tim Horton's dark roast every tenth cold call? Is it ten Jelly Belly jelly beans for every ten sales letters that go out? I suggest you take fifteen to twenty minutes and process what a win looks like for you, and if you are in an expansive mood, imagine achieving that small win and mentally drink that dark roast, or eat those jelly beans, and get your mind set up for winning!

What were your thoughts on the last chapter?

Is there something you read which you thought might benefit you if you implemented it in your life?

27

Gratitude

As I get older, I am learning more and more that people's internal states have very little to do with what is going on around them.

I am preaching to myself here as well. I have not been above a few private pity parties.

The word that seems to be cycling around right now is gratitude. I can hear the critics already.

So should I slap a stupid smile on my face when my dog dies? No, that's not what I am getting at. It is just that much of what happens to us can be positive, either in what could develop from it or in what it could teach us. There are many tools and gurus out there. Want a quick cheap way to make a difference? Use only positive self-talk for one week. Let me know what happens.

What were your thoughts on the last chapter?

Is there something you read which you thought might benefit you if you implemented it in your life?

28

Find your hidden talents and skills:

Do you know all of your talents and skills? *Unless you've spent a lot of time pondering and investigating, you have many talents and skills that may have eluded your awareness.* Some of your greatest abilities might still be a mystery to you! You can find them with a little work.

What were your thoughts on the last chapter?

Is there something you read which you thought might benefit you if you implemented it in your life?

29

Looking back

Revisit your early years. What did you like to do before you learned to care about what others thought? What did you enjoy? What were you good at? What did you want to be when you grew up? There's a good chance you'll remember a talent or two that you forgot all about.

Spend some time alone. When your surroundings change, your perspective changes. Go to the park or spend the weekend camping. Take a trip and get out of town for a couple of days. You'll generate new ideas.

Take a test. There are several personality, interest, and skill assessments available online. It's important to answer as honestly as possible if you want an accurate assessment. Take several assessments and look for commonalities. It's likely that you can determine several strengths from the areas that overlap.

Ask others what they think. Ask your closest friends and family members what they think are your greatest strengths and talents. You know things about your friends they can't see for themselves. The same is true of you. ***Be receptive to the ideas you receive.***

Make a list. Think about the amazing things you've accomplished in the past. What talents and skills did you use to make those things happen? After completing this exercise with all of your accomplishments, do you see a common theme? There's a lot to be learned from your past accomplishments.

What is unique about you? How do you stand out from your friends, family, and coworkers? What's special about you? This is another great question to ask those around you.

What do you enjoy? If you had a free afternoon to yourself, how would you spend it? Would you spend a free day working on your classic car or build an electronics project? Would you build a webpage? ***Your strengths often lie in your interests.***

What do you like to talk about? Is there something you're so passionate about that your friends wish you'd quit talking about it? Which topics do you think make for interesting conversation?

When do you lose track of time? Do you lose track of time while you're painting? Writing? Woodworking? ***The things that fully engage your mind can be related to your strengths.***

What's easy for you? What do you find easy that others find hard to do? You can do at least a few things better than just about everyone you know.

If you had to go back to school, what would you choose as your major? Math? You're probably good at math, abstract concepts, and solving problems. Creative writing? You likely have strengths in writing, reading, creativity, and imagination. What would you like to study if you had the time, money, and motivation?

What were your thoughts on the last chapter?

Is there something you read which you thought might benefit you if you implemented it in your life?

You can reach me at *wayne@waynepratt.ca*

30

What do you do when things go wrong?

I know it seems ironic, but coaches and motivators can have bad days. The key is what do when those days hit. The key is how do you keep them from becoming bad weeks or bad months. I think the biggest difference is a long term focus, and specifically a focus on your goals. This should make the setbacks seem less fatal. I think you would be wise to develop the medium term goal period. That is one to five years, If I could be more specific, twelve to eighteen months. Here is where the heavy lifting is done. Most of us get through our days, but planning, shaping the bigger picture rarely get done in the hubbub of our day.

So if today seems bleak, be gentle with yourself, and look to the future.

What were your thoughts on the last chapter?

Is there something you read which you thought might benefit you if you implemented it in your life?

31

Become an Overcomer!

You're familiar with resistance. It reveals itself every time you think about doing something new or something you don't want to do. It's that uncomfortable feeling that hits you somewhere in your stomach or your chest. ***Successfully handling resistance is important if you want to get things done.*** Those that give in to resistance are the same people that tend to struggle with life.

Resistance can strike when you're thinking about going to the gym, working on a report for work, calling the in-laws, or mowing the grass. Resistance is the feeling that leads to procrastination.

Learn to overcome your resistance and get things done:

It's just a feeling in your body. Your brain is excellent at dissuading you from doing things it considers dangerous on some level. However, resistance is nothing more than an uncomfortable feeling.

You can deal with a little mild discomfort and avoid letting it derail your plans. **Observe it.** One of the best ways to lessen the effect of resistance is to look at it objectively, like a scientist. You might think to yourself, *"Hmm, isn't that interesting? I think about going for a run and I get a slight queasy feeling high in my stomach."* Continue to observe and something interesting will happen. **The negative feeling will begin to dissipate.**

Avoid running away. The common reaction is to distract yourself. Depending on your habits, you might turn on the TV, get on the Internet, text a friend, or eat a cookie. This is a huge mistake. Just stay with your discomfort until it subsides. Running away just reinforces the pattern of allowing resistance to stop you.

Remind yourself why this task is important. What is the purpose of getting it done? A healthier body? Increased income? An attractive yard that won't offend the neighbors? Have a good reason and you'll be more motivated.

Recognize that the first step is the most challenging. Avoid thinking about sitting at your desk and working on a report for the next three hours. Instead, think about sitting down in front of the computer with a cup of coffee and typing the first word. If you're headed for the gym, your primary task is to put on your workout clothes.

Do whatever it takes to take that first step. Everything that follows is much easier. You'll often find yourself surprised by how easy the task was to complete once you got started.

Everyone deals with resistance each and every day. It's part of the human condition. We naturally avoid those things that are perceived as unpleasant. ***However, your success is limited by how much you allow resistance to rule your decisions.*** Use these strategies consistently and you'll be back in charge of your life.

What were your thoughts on the last chapter?

Is there something you read which you thought might benefit you if you implemented it in your life?

So you want to be coached?

As you consider being coached, please ask yourself if you *really* want things to change?

If you want to make life changes I'd love to help.

To find out if coaching is right for you, please contact me!

You can reach me at *wayne@waynepratt.ca*

www.ingramcontent.com/pod-product-compliance
Lightning Source LLC
Chambersburg PA
CBHW030309100526
44590CB00012B/574